Leadership That Reaches Every Student

Leadership That Reaches Every Student

◆

A Guide for Teachers and Parents Who
Are Concerned about Providing Students
with Vision & Leadership

Marcal Graham, Ed.D

iUniverse, Inc.
New York Lincoln Shanghai

Leadership That Reaches Every Student
A Guide for Teachers and Parents Who Are Concerned about Providing Students with Vision & Leadership

iUniverse books may be ordered through booksellers or by contacting:

iUniverse
2021 Pine Lake Road, Suite 100
Lincoln, NE 68512
www.iuniverse.com
1-800-Authors (1-800-288-4677)

Because of the dynamic nature of the Internet, any Web addresses or links contained in this book may have changed since publication and may no longer be valid.

The views expressed in this work are solely those of the author and do not necessarily reflect the views of the publisher, and the publisher hereby disclaims any responsibility for them.

ISBN: 978-0-595-45785-4 (pbk)
ISBN: 978-0-595-69857-8 (cloth)
ISBN: 978-0-595-90087-9 (ebk)

Printed in the United States of America

This book is dedicated to God, without whom nothing in my life would exist.

To my mother, Marion Graham, and my sister Char-juan Graham, who have been my inspiration and support system my entire life.

Sandra V. Jones, you have always been there in heart and spirit for me. I did not forget you on this one! Thanks for being there for me through the ups and downs in life. I appreciate your inner fire and spirit immensely. You are one in a million.

Kenneth Goodwin, thanks for your kind and inspirational words. You are the brother I never had.

Renee Hemsley, thank you for all our insightful and rich conversations about art, education, and life. You are truly concerned about the youth of today.

Dorrette Prince, thank you for all your help in proof-reading both of my manuscripts.

"You close the academic gap at the same time that you close the access gap, the economic gap, the employment gap ... "

Joe A. Hairston, superintendent of Baltimore County Public Schools, 2007

"Every mandate of No Child Left Behind—*and there are hundreds—is designed to force the people who run our schools to shape up, work harder, raise expectations, and stop 'making excuses' for low test scores, or face the consequences. Despite the law's oft-stated reverence for 'scientifically based research,' this narrow approach is contradicted by numerous studies documenting the importance of social and economic factors in children's academic progress."*

James Crawford, writer and lecturer, president of the Institute for Language and Educational Policy, 2007

"Higher standards, a well-designed curriculum, and exemplary instruction are of limited value unless students are engaged and motivated to learn what is taught. Until more students decide to work harder, there will be no significant improvement in our schools no matter how much better we teach."

Bob Sullo, respected educator, speaker, and researcher, 2006

"Rather than serving as the 'great equalizer' as envisioned by Horace Mann, one of the early architects of American public education, schools in the United States more often have been sites where patterns of privilege and inequality are maintained and reproduced."

Dr. Pedro Noguera, author and expert on closing the achievement gap, 2003

"Students must work harder, longer, and with more discipline and sacrifice or there will not be a place for them at the table."

Ray Esquith, teacher with over twenty years' experience teaching urban students, 2003

Contents

Preface

Many policy researchers argue that teacher quality is the biggest challenge with regard to closing the achievement gap with low-income and minority students. They consistently leave out the role that parents, and more importantly students, must play with regard to their own achievement. In addition, they do not address the school's historical role as an economic sorting mechanism that was created to reinforce and reproduce social inequality. How can school systems transform the lives of students if their main goal is to perform the opposite function?

Historically, schools have served one function: to reproduce the status-quo economically, socially, and educationally. For students in many low-income and racially diverse communities to have a fighting chance, they must aspire to excellence. Academic excellence has no color, ethnicity, or race; it is simply a tool, and it can be transformative if we understand and channel it properly. Schools must teach more than reading, mathematics, and content coursework to students from urban communities. In their support of authentic assessments, Di Martino and Castaneda (2007, page 38), contend, "The United States' national obsession with core content proficiency is distracting us from teaching the skills that all graduates need for success." They go on to assert that we are not teaching—much less testing—the skills that are most needed and valued once students step into the job market. Educational theorists such as Gardner (2006) and Marx (2006) also provide support for this argument in their research.

In his book, *Five Minds for the Future* (2006), Howard Gardner discusses how as a society we must cultivate students' minds to be disciplined, to synthesize, to demonstrate creativity, to be respectful, and to be ethical as they prepare for the myriad changes of a global economy. In addition, Gary Marx in the book *Future-Focused Leadership* (2006) discusses how students will need skills that prepare them to think globally about real-world problems with far-reaching consequences.

Even more striking, the *Journal of Educational Leadership* (April 2007) ranks the skills that employers will look for in employees over the next five years as (1) critical thinking/problem solving, (2) information technology, (3) teamwork/collaboration, (4) creativity/innovation, (5) diversity, and (6) leadership (Levine 2007). According to the study, mathematics, writing, foreign language, and reading comprehension were ranked toward the bottom. I can only assume that employers expect students to come in the door having mastered such basics. However, if one examines standardized test data in many urban schools (in the nation's capital and other urban cities) one finds just the opposite occurring in terms of the lack of mastery of core content material. Even when one examines student preparation for the educational demands of higher education, one finds that many students will be ill prepared due to disagreement between what k-12 classrooms teach and what colleges and universities expect of incoming students. According to Conley (2007), students will need to be able conduct research and analysis on a much deeper and richer level than high school has prepared them for in the past.

Moreover, students need to be more proactive in demonstrating intervention (i.e., leadership) strategies to excel beyond "have not" educational status. Clearly, there are systems in place that reinforce structures and processes that impede social mobility, and at the individual level there are students who must not only dream success, but must also achieve it. This requires stepping out of their comfort zone of race, class, and gender, and transcending the low expectations that society has for them.

Therefore, the power to change a student's social reality can come only from within—a challenge many teachers confront daily in the classroom. On students' hierarchy of needs, often times education is not viewed as self-actualizing, or even near the top of their agenda, making this challenge even greater. The goal of many public schools is not to reach the inner motivation and spirit of the student beyond achieving AYP (Adequate Yearly Progress) as many students have found out. Each year, schools must basically bribe students through incentives into showing up on the day of standardized testing and hope that they perform near their best academically. While measuring academic growth is an important endeavor, we must not neglect to provide a framework for understanding the whole student and the dynamics that affect learning.

Moreover, it is difficult to imagine that if students lack vision for the future and the global world that we are a part of, they will go into standardized testing with the attitude of expecting excellence. Unfortunately, we do our students a disservice by failing to tell them the truth. Tutoring mandated under *No Child Left Behind* will unlikely offset a poor attitude, poor behavior, and weak academic preparation. There are no magic bullets if we are not truly to attack the achievement gap plaguing public schools across the country, but there are silver linings that we must uncover, one layer at a time, to ensure that students and communities are not left behind permanently.

Introduction

This is for parents and teachers who want to nurture and plant the seeds of positive leadership in students irrespective of class, race, gender, or ethnicity. It is very difficult to hold students accountable for their actions if we do not provide the proper food and nutrients for positive thought and action. Although some of the current literature lays the responsibility for academic achievement at the feet of teachers, I assert that students must hold up their end of the bargain in order to be successful in life, as well as in the classroom. Therefore, the purpose of this book is to enable teachers and parents to inspire hope in students. Consequently, students must understand that leadership equals the sum of their daily thoughts and actions over time.

The <u>workbook</u> format is a critical one for communication among students, parents, and teachers. Centered on the student, its purpose is to dismantle the barriers that students never conquer with traditional textbooks.

This is an ongoing series that attempts to provide students with a blueprint for how to overcome academic, personal, and social obstacles.

Chapter 1, "Can We Make Public Schools Transformational?" is a comprehensive view of schools and the role they must play as we move forward as a society.

Chapter 2, "The Path of Least Resistance," deeply examines the role that parents must play in promoting academic achievement and accountability in the lives of their children.

Chapter 3, "Leadership and Positive Decision Making" reveals how students should assume leadership if they are to overcome many of life's obstacles as they travel throughout the maze of life.

Chapter 4, "Academic Leadership and Follow-Through," asks students whether they are really ready to take the next step toward leadership.

Chapter 5, "Leadership and Higher Education 101," addresses the concept of leadership and higher education.

Chapter 6, "The Importance of Time and Leadership," explores the challenges that students face in dealing with the demands of time and maintaining leadership over their lives.

Chapter 7, "Vision," will help students determine the role that vision will have in their short and long-term future.

Chapter 8, "Who Are the Anti-Leaders" addresses the role that negative peer pressure has on student leadership.

Chapter 9, "Conclusion: What does it All Mean?" summarizes the role that students must play to be effective leaders. It looks at the types of actions and behaviors that undermine leadership development at all levels. We know that students resist being viewed as leaders and we need to understand the factors that affect positive and negative peer interaction.

Instructions on Administrating the Leadership Survey

When administering surveys researchers rarely collect enough rich data that addresses underlying root causes. Whether students are truly aware of their actions and behaviors cannot be surmised from a typical quantitative survey instrument and therefore we must develop a survey that captures their total experiences qualitatively. This survey should be administered to students in a classroom setting or as a graded leadership project so they can understand how important their responses are to actual teaching and learning. The responses are meant to be shared individually and collectively so that students and teachers understand the expectations and gaps that may exist between the two groups. Eventually, we will want to share these results with parents personally at parent-teacher conferences so that they can also ascertain the attitudes, behaviors, and experiences that their children are going through as they navigate school, home, and life. The overall goal of this survey is to bring together in dialogue groups (i.e., teachers, students, parents) who usually do not talk to one another enough about students assuming leadership roles together.

Teachers should allow students as much time as necessary to complete the leadership survey which can be administered over the course of a week in order to make sure students remain engaged in the activity. Moreover, students should be graded on their ability to reflect critically on their past and current experiences and explain how leadership touches their lives. As with most writing projects, there are no right or wrong answers to these questions, but students must take the time to actually form their thoughts. No prior training or classes on leadership are necessary to take this survey.

Leadership Survey

Part I. Leadership Survey

1. I believe that I have some leadership qualities. Agree/Disagree. Please list and explain.

2. I do not think that leadership is that important. Agree/Disagree. Explain.

3. Do situations determine who are leaders rather than people? Yes or No. Explain.

4. What are some of the challenging aspects of being a leader? Are you ready for those challenges?

5. I can follow someone and still take leadership over my thoughts and actions. Agree/Disagree. Explain.

6. What needs to happen to you in order for you to become an effective leader?

7. When can being a follower be bad for your health, grades, and future? Provide some examples of when

you followed a friend or family member and something negative happened?

8. How do you demonstrate leadership to yourself, your family, and your friends? How has it made you a better person?

9. Name a time when a person in a leadership position disappointed you.

10. What scares you about assuming leadership in school and around you friends?

11. Does being a leader require effort or does it come to you naturally? Explain.

12. What leadership skills do you hide from your friends?

Part II. Leadership Survey

13. What bad habits of a leader do you demonstrate? For example, are you vain, bossy, too talkative?

14. How important is discipline to good leadership?

15. What kind of classes in your school would you feel comfortable being a leader in?

16. What leadership skills have you picked up from your teachers?

17. List some of the reasons why you choose to follow people?

18. When you make a decision(s) do you think about the ramifications? Yes or No. Please Explain.

19. If you had to name one person in your life whom you thought was a leader in your life who would that person be? Why did you choose this person?

20. With 1 being the lowest and 10 being the highest, rank your ability to lead people. Why did you give yourself that score?

21. What does it take for you to make a good decision? What is your process?

22. Bonus question. How many good and bad decisions did you make today? Give examples of some and explain why they were good or bad.

1

Can We Make Public Schools Transformational?

INTRODUCTION

This chapter examines student performance on standardized examinations and the educational value these tests have on student achievement. One of the underlying issues in this chapter is students' willingness to assume responsibility for their performance. Although schools have become more data-driven under No Child Left Behind (NCLB) *performance targets, they have failed to address underlying issues that continue to plague student academic growth. Another question posed in this chapter speaks to the role and impact of* NCLB. *Understanding these dynamics is paramount to closing the achievement gap plaguing many public schools.*

I often wonder if students realize who their role models are when they are adolescents and young adults. Many students say their parents, grandparents, teachers, friends, and even successful athletes are their role models. While all of these people have an impact and role in our development, eventually the student must take the lead. The challenge to students is to take time to think about why they willingly follow the behaviors of others rather than reflecting on who they are as people. Sometimes you may have to reflect or reconsider as to whether you should follow a person, especially if a negative outcome is possible. In addition, helping students see the big picture is even more important because many students seem to live life piecemeal, unable to see that they must have a vision of their futures in order to reach it.

Standardized testing only represents only a small part of their educational experience. The "big picture" is understanding that if you are engaged in learning then you must give over one hundred percent of yourself to the process. The end result is a reflection of all those hours, days, and weeks that were spent learning and re-learning your craft. At that point, learning has become part of you and will never leave you. It is only after you have given all of yourself to the academic process that tutoring and extra instruction become necessary and effective.

Data from National Assessment for Educational Progress (NAEP) continues to demonstrate that students are not performing on grade level, much less at their true academic potential. According to 2005 NAEP data, a quarter of the nation's high school seniors lack basic reading skills, and over 40 percent even lack mathematical skills. Unfortunately, this number is worst for low-income and minority students (Paley, 2007). It appears that testing for the sake of testing is not a prudent or effective way for schools to motivate student academic success. In the book, *Activating the Desire to Learn* (2007, 155), Sullo states, "Even though students are doing better on the high-stakes tests (a function of teachers 'teaching to the test'), they have failed to improve with regard to other measures, such as the National Assessment of Educational Progress page 155." This is troubling since many states, schools, and school districts are not judged proficient under *NCLB* if they do not reach certain proficiency benchmarks in reading and mathematics.

An April 5, 2007, US Department of Education study that was released in the *Washington Post* stated that much of the educational software that schools (especially urban underperforming schools) use to close the achievement gap, was ineffective. According to researchers, they evaluated 15 reading and mathematics computer programs used by 9,424 students in 132 schools across the country during the 2004-2005 school year. They compared standardized test scores of students who used the treatment with those students who did not. Unfortunately, the findings demonstrated no statistically significant differences between the two groups of students tested.

While it is discouraging that many students are not performing up to their academic abilities, more troubling is the fact that the billions of dollars that schools have invested in educational software have not helped to close learning gaps. In addition, there appears to be little innovation to address these deficiencies beyond these educational software programs to improve standardized test scores. Unfortunately, I see and live this reality everyday in the charter school where I work in Washington DC. Right now, it appears that the educational system is an exercise in futility, at least on the front lines. If one takes the quotes at the beginning of this book at face value, it would seem that much of the power to change their educational realities lies with students.

With the advent of high school graduation examinations, advanced placement tests, and International Baccalaureate courses, students will need to demonstrate high levels of academic discipline or risk being left behind academically. Under *NCLB*, schools that are designated as "In Need of Improvement" must set aside a portion of their Title 1 money for supplemental educational services or tutoring. While this is a noble deed, tutoring is only one part of the equation; the other part is student motivation and effort. According to Grossman (2007), "The Chicago Public Schools spent $50 million in federal money on after school tutoring for 56,000 students last year but test scores show it got limited bang for its buck." (page 1) The data demonstrate that tutored elementary students in reading and negligible results in mathematics when compared to eligible students who did not take advantage of the additional tutoring services.

Character Education and *NCLB*

Character education programs often function diametrically opposite to the goals of *NCLB*. Under *NCLB* all students must be proficient in reading, mathematics, and science by 2013-14. One of the many goals of *NCLB* is to ensure that all students are able to reach academic targets irrespective of race, gender, economic class, or language deficiency. Consequently, *NCLB* has been concerned with accountability and meeting state learning standards. Unfortunately, the program has not accounted for the following truth:

"If character is the thought, then leadership is the action"

NCLB does not address character or leadership development in students. These goals should be identical; many people view them as mutually exclusive. I believe that character and leadership function alongside and feed off each other. More specifically, I assert that if character is the thought then leadership is the action that is needed for decisions to take place. At the heart is determining the best and most effective strategy to educate students to perform on grade level. Instilling character in students is not a new concept, but developing the skills and the attitude toward learning are even more important to the overall academic growth of a student.

Can schools be data driven and nurture character at the same time? I believe the answer is yes, but with one important caveat. If schools cannot create strategies to motivate students then they certainly will wage a losing battle to improve student achievement. Clearly, students cannot assume that all parents will be willing participants on the educational battlefield. Unfortunately, some parents will be casualties of life and some will be missing in action. Consequently, we need an intervention that is transformative and holistic in scope. What we have not been able to do is to marry the two forces that affect the education of students; we must emphasize thought and action in order to directly impact behavior. I think leadership that transforms a student's attitude is a key ingredient in improving student achievement. Character does not need to be taught separately from other core content classes, but that academic excellence should be emphasized school-wide. In my experience, academic excellence and undertakings will instill character-building skills in students. So the question that one must ask is how do you drive academic excellence and intrinsic motivation within students?

In the article "U.S. Rates Full Set of Character Education Programs," the U.S. Department of Education (Viadero, 2007)) examined and ranked some of the most effective character-based education programs across the country. The study included a checklist of criteria to determine the effectiveness of a program. The areas are as follows:

- Improving behaviors
- Enhancing students' moral and ethical reasoning or their attitudes and values
- Gaining in academic achievement

I strongly believe that any successful character-based program should have some measurable criteria for determining its impact on learning and more importantly on whether it has changed the way students view themselves and the world around them. Leadership development forces students to re-evaluate their actions, attitude, and the amount of effort they are bring to any undertaking academic or otherwise. From an academic standpoint, we would have to examine quantitative measures such as attendance rates, lateness, and test scores. Conversely, we would need to also assess qualitative measures such as public speaking, student/teacher interactions, and behaviors inside and outside (i.e., cafeteria or after school) of the classroom changed over time. In addition, one might examine whether students cut classes less often or whether their perceptions of self changed significantly after acquiring leadership skills. If this occurs then learning has the potential to become transformative. While this may seem like a daunting process, it is critical that teachers document and challenge students beyond academic performance on standardized test scores.

TRANSFORMATIONAL LEADERSHIP

I was interviewing for an assistant professor's position at a university in the Midwest two years ago when the search committee asked me a question about what I thought transformative leadership was. The first idea that came to mind was that it was a way to inspire people to follow you. I was taken aback when they asked for a deeper and richer explanation of the term. So I thought a little deeper and defined "transformative leadership" as seeking information beyond just knowing, but wanting to know so that one can impact one's community, economic condition, and social standing. Bernard Bass and Ronald Riggio (2006) define transformative leadership as the ability to "stimulate and inspire followers to both achieve extraordinary outcomes, and in the process, develop their own leadership capacity." (page 3) Moreover, transformational leaders are able to motivate others to do more than they thought possible according to Bass & Riggio (2006).

In addition, Bass and Riggio assert that transformational leaders provide an environment where people grow and feel a sense of empowerment which is connected to the objectives of the overall mission of the leader or organization. Conversely, there is transactional leadership, where individuals seek leadership through the exchange of financial rewards or goods and services. If we look at schools today, we see that many of them operate from a reward-based position. Under *NCLB*, schools, administrators, teachers, and to a lesser degree students are rewarded for their performance on certain benchmark examinations. If they fail to meet a certain performance plateaus they are punished financially and run the risk of more punitive actions being assessed.

How do these actions foster better schools or better students? Although we recognize the need for ways to measure learning, is this the most productive way to do this?

If we re-examine schools in the lens of transformational and transactional leadership, we see the need for programs and interventions that incorporate these elements. For example, after-school programs must offer incentives that students find enriching and enjoyable (e.g., stipends, exposure to cultural arts, social etiquette classes, and sporting events) and that build leadership and cultural capital that provides students with the tools to help themselves and their communities. Moreover, students must see education as something with immediate value that fosters their growth and transformation.

According to Marzano (2003, 144), "If students are motivated to learn the content in a given subject, their achievement in that subject will likely be good. Conversely," he says, "if students are not motivated to learn the content, their achievement will likely be limited." Student achievement does not simply rest in the hands of teachers only, but must involve students and parents who are critical to academic growth. According to Sullo

(2007, 156), "We have been unsuccessful in our attempt to motivate more students to achieve academically and behave responsibly because we have based our efforts on the mistaken belief that people can be externally motivated to do their best work. In truth, we are motivated within." Therefore, the kinds of questions we need to pose should be more reflective, qualitative, and student driven.

What level of motivation are you bringing into the classroom? For example, what about the fifth grade student who hands in four out of ten homework assignments to the teacher even after the teacher has called home and spoken with the parent or guardian after the first and second uncompleted assignment? The responsibility cannot rest solely at the feet of teachers, but students must at some point be accountable for their actions.

Discussion Question for Parents and Teachers

- What does it mean to be transformational?
- What comes first: good leadership or good character? Can you have one without the other? Why?

- Based on the research, what do you think is the best way to motivate students?

2

The Path of Least Resistance

"The only way for students to overcome the shortcomings of their parents is for them to take the lead in their own future."

Chapter 2 examines the challenges that parents encounter in raising their children and the role they must play. One of the many goals of this chapter is to develop a dialogue between parents and teachers to discuss the many problems that impact teaching and learning. We need solutions that have short- and long-term benefits for student learning. Understanding how teachers and parents can close any gaps in communicating is an ongoing problem that many schools need to address if they are to attack their academic problems.

Talking to many people in educational circles, it is hard to determine if parents and teachers are friends or foes. The relationship appears to be strained at best and adversarial at worst. How did we get to the point where many parents neglect or fail to follow through on student learning? Even when teachers present convincing evidence—academic, behavioral, or otherwise—many parents tend to dismiss it altogether. It is almost as if the student can do nothing wrong and that teachers need corroborating video footage to reinforce their argument. Conversely, teachers have a habit of dismissing the views and experiences of parents, especially those who appear and sound less educated.

Parents play a very critical role in how students view themselves, especially as leaders. I do not feel for one moment that leaders are born; they must be nurtured and guided into understanding that their must make decisions that have lasting consequences. We also found that many parents neglect to instill these ideas in their own children because they lacked either leadership or direction themselves. Parents have a myriad of reasons for not taking the initiative in the lives of their children. There are socioeconomic class issues. Sometimes food, entertainment, and childcare are not enough to entice parents into the school building for open-house events and parent-teachers conferences. Therefore, we must give parents the room and time to see that we are on the same team and want the best for their children. In other words, a better message might be, "In teachers we trust, rather than in the words of children," who have their own reasons and agenda for not completing homework or studying for an examination.

Another issue that divides the two groups is communication about the real problems affecting teaching and learning. An apparent problem is the inability of parents to actually develop strategies at home that reinforce positive behavior in the classroom. It seems as if students go home and care very little of about what they have learned in the classroom. Conversely, they seem to take many of the problems and habits from home into the classroom.

Many parents want to be their child's friend first and parent second. This will not and cannot work when disruptive students develop strategies of resistance and refuse to listen to teachers in the classroom, especially with regard to learning. Unfortunately, many parents validate this behavior allowing the student to think that this negative and success-undermining behavior has a place in the classroom or in society overall. If parents ask the right questions on student behavior and attitude we can start to change in the perceptions of students who think they can manipulate their parents and teachers.

The following section poses questions that are critical to understanding the challenges that parents have in raising their children. Parents need to be aware that their direct and indirect actions speak volumes to their children. Therefore, they must model and demonstrate that they fully support academic and personal excellence in the classroom. This can only happen if parents ask students engaging questions about learning as well as reflect on the role they have had in helping to build stronger relationships with schools and teachers.

Reflective Questions for Parent Reflection

- What did you learn today? What skill did you gain today in reading and math? Explain.

- How much time do you spend reading a day?

- What new vocabulary words did you learn this week?

- Are you too tired to talk with your child once you get home from work? Yes or No.

- Are you contributing to your child's dislike of school through your own behavior?

- Have you attempted to build a relationship with your child's teacher(s)?

- When was the last time you had a positive connection with one of your child's teachers?

- How often do you spend time in the library with your child?

- How can schools better assist you in educating your child?

- What type of parent organization would you join if you had the time?

- What are some of the challenges you must overcome in order to raise your child?

- What separates a good parent from a bad parent? What are you doing daily to be a good parent?

- Do you have an adversarial relationship with any of your child's teachers?

Questions for Student Reflection

Students must realize that they are part of the solution and must therefore reflect on their role in learning inside and outside the classroom. Consequently, they must be prepared to think deeply about their reality and the power they have to shape and re-shape their future.

- What problems have you faced in reading and math? What are you doing about them?

- Are you honest about the role you have played in your academic success? Please explain.

- Can you name some educational obstacles you have not been able to overcome?

- How do you deal with personal obstacles in your life?

- Do you allow personal obstacles to interfere with your work in school?

- Have you ever allowed personal problems to hold you back in your life?

- How do you view failure? Is it a positive or negative? Is it temporary or permanent? Can failure be a good thing? Has it ever motivated you to try harder?

- Is your thinking the problem? Are your actions part of the problem?

- What do you think about the following statement by John Maxwell (2007)?
  "Those who see the problem and because they didn't personally create them are content to blame someone else."

- Have you ever identified a problem and done nothing about it? Name a situation when this happened.

Discussion Question for Parents and Teachers

a) From this chapter did you gain a better understanding of the challenges that teachers and parents face daily?

b) What have you done to make parents/teachers friends or foes? Do you have a defensive posture or are you open to constructive feedback?

c) <u>For parents</u>: Have you ever reflected on your parenting skills?

d) <u>For teachers</u>: Have you ever reflected on your teaching skills?

3

Leadership and Positive Decision Making

There are defining moments and times when you must assume leadership over the decisions you make in your life. The fact is that these decisions happen every day.

This chapter provides questions and activities that support positive student decision making as it pertains to leadership development. The aim is for students to gain a deeper understanding of the daily challenges that shape them as individuals and the consequences of their decisions. Moreover, students must understand that their decisions should be well thought out and not impulsive in nature.

<u>LEADERSHIP DECISION MAKING</u>

- There are multiple avenues to leadership that we take each day. As a leader, you determine your path during the day and night many times, without even thinking about it. This can have short- and long-term repercussions on your future and options you will have.

- What is negative student peer pressure? How do you handle it? Does it prevent you from becoming a leader?

- Can peer pressure be positive? Explain.

According to James Kouzes and Barry Posner (2002) in the book the <u>Leadership Challenge</u>, leaders must engage in five practices of exemplary leadership. Please rank the following from 1 to 5 with 1 being the most important to leadership and 5 being the least important. It might be helpful to define each term before you rank them.

- Model the way   ____

- Inspire a shared vision   ____

- Challenge the process   ____

- Enable others to act   ____

- Encourage the heart   ____

What do these leadership practices mean to you? What was your first pick? Why? What do you think is the least important? Have you ever shared your vision for the future with someone?

In the article, "Why Should Anyone Be Led by You," Robert Goffee and Gareth Jones (2000) in their discussion of inspirational leaders state that one of the qualities that leaders need to share is their ability to demonstrate weakness or vulnerability in order to build trust. They go on to further assert, "Sharing an imperfection is so effective because it underscores a human being's authenticity" (page 46). Do you agree with this? What does this mean to you and your ability to lead? Have you ever shared an imperfection with someone?

If you had to develop a leadership academy/school for you and your friends what would your leadership academy look like? How would you inspire your friends to give their best? How would you get them to come to school every day? What kind of teachers would you hire? How would you inspire a shared vision and culture in your school?

4

Academic Leadership and Follow-Through

Many of us are guilty of talking a good game when discussing what we would do if we were in a particular situation. Unfortunately, few of us have the follow-through to make our dreams come true. We make excuses and blame others for our inability to take the lead and "follow-through" with the dreams we have for ourselves. I introduced the concept of leadership follow-through in my first book Seeing the Need and Choosing to Lead *(2006).*

Those familiar with the sport of basketball understand free-throw shooting and how a player must bend his knees and be mechanically sound as the ball leaves his hands. The same process is true for tennis where one must always be in the ready position with the racket face back, legs bent, and feet facing the net.

When we apply this concept to student learning and leadership we find that students are often indifferent to preparation and attempt to shortcut the mechanics of excellence. This happens too much in the classroom where students attempt to circumvent the process of excellence when it comes to their growth and academic development. Can students overcome poor academic mechanics (i.e., preparation) with less than a full commitment to completing the goals in front of them? For those who come from family backgrounds of economic privilege there is a strong likelihood that they will be provided opportunities (i.e., social capital and social networks) to offset inadequate preparation and planning. Conversely, those who come from families with limited exposure to other cultures and economic classes find it extremely difficult to close the achievement gap.

For example, to make academic gains and master content in mathematics and reading students need to build fundamental skills. I do not believe that excellence is possible without a proper work ethic. It is very hard to imagine that one can be successful without the proper foundation for learning. Excellence is a byproduct of a good attitude and work habits which work hand and hand. To have two out of three is not good enough if students are trying to compete in a global society.

The Mechanics of Excellence

- **Do you feel like you possess excellence?**
- **What will it take for you to achieve excellence?**

- **What will it take for you to maintain excellence?**

In the book, *Seeing the Need and Choosing to Lead* (2007), I touched on the concept of leadership follow-through and how students fail to understand how sports and learning mirror one another. There is a regimen of excellence and hard work that one must undergo in sports in order to be the best. The same holds true in the classroom where students must study and commit time and mental energy until they have mastered the course material. In examining this concept, I have expounded on the fact that in order for students to truly master their respective classes they must take leadership and ownership over their learning. When I reflect on how I was able to overcome personal, academic, and professional challenges as a child growing up, I am reminded of how I had to sacrifice, examine the implications of my choices, and relentlessly pursue excellence. I had to take the lead, not my mother, not my teachers, not my community, but me.

Questions for Student Reflection

a) What did you learn from this chapter?

b) What do your mechanics of excellence look like?

5

Leadership and Higher Education 101

"Students don't start becoming leaders once they arrive at the door steps of college. In many ways it is too late because the race started the minute they walked into first grade."

This chapter addresses the various challenges that students in colleges and universities face as they transition from high school to higher learning. The goal is to bridge the leadership gap so that students have a starting point which allows them to reflect on situations in which they must take the lead academically and socially. Geared toward college students, the chapter illustrates the needs and concerns that students attending college will encounter and the role that leadership will have in their negotiating positive outcomes. The situations presented are ones in which they must assume leadership in higher education or risk facing negative consequences.

Higher education is about finding the leadership within you. At every level you are expected to assume leadership over your learning. One can seek leadership in groups by joining fraternities, or sororities, or student government or by possibly joining or starting your own student organizations. In addition, students must navigate through financial aid needs. You are always challenged in college to seek leadership and make choices in the classroom, with friends, and among family. Do I go home to visit family the weekend before a major examination which could determine my final grade? Is it just easier to be a follower and play it safe? Once students finish college they must take the lead in order to find employment or pursue additional education such as law, medicine, or graduate school.

Discussion Questions for College-Level Students

- What does leadership mean to you?

- On a scale of 1-10 with 10 being the highest, and 1 the lowest rank your capacity or ability to be a leader. Explain why you ranked yourself at that particular number.

- According to Jonathan Kozol (2005, 11) in the book, *The Shame of The Nation*, in his discussion of apartheid schooling in the United States, Kozol states, "What saddens me the most during these times is simply that these children have no knowledge of the other world in which I've lived most of my life and that the children in that other world have not the slightest notion as to who these children are and will not likely ever know them later on, not at least on anything like equal terms, unless a couple of these kids get into college." What does this mean to you?

- Are you a quiet leader?

- What is the difference between an emerging and seasoned leader?

- How do you handle the various personalities of your teachers/professors? What about when they are boring?

- What activities have you been doing to build trust in your personal relationships?

- Can you afford to miss a class lecture? Some students seem to be able to miss a class lecture and not miss a beat while others fall further and further behind. How do you prevent this from happening?

- Many students seem to not want to meet students outside of their comfort zone and miss some wonderful experiences. How do you prevent this from happening? Discuss some times when you stepped outside of your comfort zone.

- Where is the most productive place for you to get work done? Please circle.

    - Library

    - Cafeteria

    - Your dorm

    - With friends

    - Watching television in your dorm room or campus apartment

    - Listening to Your mp3 player in the student activities center

- You have a group project with three people in your class, but two members always seem to come approximately fifteen minutes to late to each meeting. One member came to the past two meetings unprepared with their portion of the work. How do you handle this situation as a leader?

- Do you know the various ways one can withdraw from a class? If you had to withdraw from a class, what are some of the steps you would have to take in order to withdraw?

- How does a course syllabus function like a contract? What must leaders do before they act or make decisions?

- How would you handle an academic progress report that said you were failing a particular class?

- Are you able to manage your time effectively? What are some of the demands placed on your time?

- Are you afraid to admit when you are lost in a class? Has your pride ever prevented you from asking for extra help? What does asking for help have to do with leadership?

- Can you really expect to ace a chemistry or calculus class by cramming? How often to do you find yourself cramming for class?

- You have a major test to study for tonight and two of your friends have just asked to attend one of the biggest games of the year against your school's divisional rival. In addition, they have a couple of kegs of beer for before and after the game. You have been in similar situations and managed to earn B's. If you do not pass this exam with a B or better you run the risk of falling below the 3.0 threshold and thus jeopardizing your chances of being on the dean's list. How do you handle this situation?

• Young women tend to take their work a lot more seriously than young men in college. Please circle True or False, and explain.

• Friday nights are the best time to study. Please circle True or False.

• What do you drink to keep you awake as you prepare for a night of cramming?

• Have you found that working out in the gym helps you deal with stress? Please circle True or False.

• What do you talk about with your mentor?

The library is a great place to:

> • Pick up members of the opposite sex
>
> • Study
>
> • Sleep

- Engage in intellectually stimulating conversations with one's self and friends

- All the above

- How much sleep do you need in order to get up for a full day of work and or school?

- How did you prepare for your SATs?

  - Take a prep course

  - Study on your own with an SAT textbook

- One of the benefits of college life is that you gain freedom to do many things with your spare time. Name some of the activities that provide an outlet for you.

- Name some ways in which you have grown as a person in your higher education years.

- Do you think your parents understand how stressful college life is? Please circle Yes or No.

- How are teamwork, collaboration, and leadership similar in sports and in the classroom?

- How has your attitude influenced your vision for leadership?

- What is the biggest difference between being a leader in high school and college?

- Being a leader in many cases requires jettisoning certain bad habits and behaviors in order to gain mastery of one's attitude, academic potential, and overall approach to life. Are their any instances when you had to let go of some "bad habits"?

- How do you rebound when you have not done you best on an examination?

- What did you learn about yourself in this chapter?

- Are you ready to change anything about yourself?

- What events in your life have helped you to become a leader?

6

The Importance of Time and Leadership

"You are a reflection of the time you have put into yourself."

We must all make decisions under time constraints. We do not have an infinite amount of time to prepare for challenges professionally or personally. In other words, we must use time wisely and effectively if positive change is to take hold. This chapter poses questions that address how students use their time and the level of motivation they bring to the classroom. To stay ahead of time, one must take leadership over how one reacts to certain situations and events.

Discussion Questions for Students

- Take a moment to think about the value you place on time and how valuable it is to you.

- Time is one of the few things we have some form of control over, especially as a teenager and student.

- Why is time such a valuable commodity to you as a student?

- As a student, one may not have lots of money, but one does possess lots of time. How much is time worth to you? For example, let's say you have eight hours a day to do whatever you please. How would you spend your day? Would you perform the same activities every day or is your routine different day by day? Are you guilty of wasting time?

- How do you react when people make mistakes around you? Do you coach them on how not make the same mistake? Do you take the time to provide constructive feedback?

- What drives you to do your best other than money and praise?

- Do your parents motivate or de-motivate you? Please provide examples.

- Do your friends motivate or de-motivate you? Please explain.

- What are some de-motivating behaviors that continue to hold you back from greatness?

- What do you do in your spare time? How are you using it wisely?

- Are/were you afraid of being a freshman in college? How do/did you handle this fear?

- Have you ever been in part of a group project and pre-judged someone's performance based on his or her race, gender, or appearance? Name a time when you pre-judged someone's abilities based on perception.

- Do you always conform to rules? Have you broken any rules in your life? Did you ever break rules for a good purpose?

- What did you learn about yourself and how you use time?

7
Vision

"Having vision is like having a compass; without it you are lost."

This chapter introduces students to the concept of vision and the role it has in their lives. Oftentimes, students fail to realize that they control the outcomes of the decisions they make. If they dedicated themselves to developing proper long-term planning and goal-setting then many would dramatically increase their chances of success in the classroom and in life. For this to happen, students must create a blueprint that demonstrates the proper thought and action necessary to overcome personal, academic, and social barriers.

Vision allows you to see past immediate limitations and provides a framework for determining the best decision or choice to make in any given situation. Unfortunately, many of our students only think about the here and now and fail to adequately plan for their future at any level. They do not anticipate unforeseen changes and neglect to set goals in the short and long-term. Without vision students are unable to take the lead and fall prey to the forces of good and bad in the larger society. More specifically, students need vision to overcome many of the societal barriers they will encounter. While it is not a panacea for overcoming every social, economic, and educational ill that one can imagine it does allow students to see beyond their immediate surroundings and reach for something deeper and more meaningful.

Discussion Questions <u>for Students</u>

- What does it mean to have a vision?

- Imagine you had no vision for the future. What would you do with your life? Can you live your life without having a vision for the future?

- Who in your family has demonstrated vision? What about your friends?

- What do you want to accomplish today? Over the next three months? Six months? What can you accomplish in the next month?

- Name a personal trait (e.g., trusting people, laziness, getting upset over small things, self-confidence) that you are having a problem dealing with.

- What things in your life do you have control over?

- What are some things in your life that you have control over?

- Vision-building is taking life one-step-at a time. Are you moving vertically or horizontally? In other words, are you moving away from or towards your goals?

- You must make a choice to take responsibility for your actions and attitude. If your attitude were money how much would you have earned today?

- What have you learned about your vision?

- What impact does having a vision have on your short and long-term future?

- Can you name some people you would consider to be visionaries?

- How do you help a person to develop a vision?

8

Who Are the Anti-Leaders?

"You will never maximize your potential if you follow negative people."

Peer pressure is not a new phenomenon, but it remains one that can impair students' ability to assume leadership. Students are often recipients of negative peer pressure and leadership. Consequently, understanding the dynamics of how students promote negative behavior in school is very important and it is the focus of this chapter.

Unfortunately, students follow behind others even when their behavior is detrimental to their personal, intellectual, and emotional health and well-being. This happens so often to students who put their academic lives in the hands of people who they assume are their friends. As educators, we must ask students to think deeply about the kinds of relationships they are forming inside and outside of the classroom. What makes a person a friend or someone you should follow? How do students differentiate between students who have their best interests at heart and those who merely bring down their level of positive energy and attitude?

Think about who you consider to be a friend/friends and list the reasons why they are considered friends.

What are their qualities? Do they push you toward leadership? Do you find yourself always following them? Have you ever stood up for yourself? The following list below ("What Are Anti-Leaders?") provides a breakdown of the kinds of issues and questions teachers need to pose to students so that they view leadership as a positive undertaking. Unfortunately, many students are affected by peers who undermine their leadership potential. I have termed these people "anti-leaders." These peers are classified as "anti-leaders."

Many students fail to realize that you can be a leader without compromising who you are as a person or the principles have instilled in you. This means standing alone on particular issues and in difficult situations, choices that have short- and long-term implications. Students must use leadership as a tool of empowerment and education. Leadership is not something to try in the classroom on one day out of the week, but is ongoing and becomes a part of you as you grow into adulthood. The list below outlines characteristics of those who are "anti-leaders."

What are Anti-Leaders?
Anti-leaders are those who ...

- Tend to be followers rather than leaders.

- Value negative peer pressure.

- Do not believe that they can be smart, build positive relationships, and be popular at the same time.

- Take pleasure in seeing friends fail at attaining their goals.

- Are only concerned with immediate gratification.

- Would rather invest in making others feel bad about themselves rather than in uplifting people around them.

- Feel very comfortable ordering teammates around on the basketball and football fields as well as other sports, but fail to assume leadership over their learning in the classroom.

Questions for Student Reflection

- How many anti-leaders have you come across in your life? What made them Anti-Leaders?

- Have you allowed them to hold you back?

- How have you dealt with them?

- Have you compromised your belief system to be part of the anti-leader crowd?

- How can you rise above anti-leaders?

Leadership Training: First Phase for Re-Engaging Students & Closing the Leadership Gap

If you want to be an effective leader you should follow these instructions to the letter.

W Want all Students to View Themselves as Leaders

E Engage Students to develop Tangible and Real-Time Solutions

B Build Effective decision-making Skills

E Every Action Has a Reaction

T Think Critically at All Times

U Understand the Consequences of your Actions

C Create Attitudes that Reinforce Positive Behavior

LEADERS.......................................

If you missed it "WE BET U C Leaders ..."

9

Conclusion: What does it All Mean?

No one single denominator makes a person a leader, but moreover it is the sum of how a person utilizes time, reflects on one's family background, confronts negative people, learns from mistakes, handles adversity, determines short-term versus long-term goals, builds vision, and strives for personal and academic excellence.

Students need teachers and parents at every turn in order to deal with the many pitfalls and quicksand that can pull a student's positive spirit down severely limiting his or her life chances. As I have outlined in this book, this is an ongoing process that begins early in life and extends into adulthood. More specifically, leadership is about making positive choices and making the most of what life offers you whether good or bad. In life we will all follow someone at some time or another which itself is neither bad nor good. The questions we must ask are why are we following this person or road? Where will it take us today and tomorrow?

Leadership is a state of mind and a function of the attitude, motivation, and actions one brings to learning and life. Students must realize that they have the ability and the power to shape and re-shape their lives through positive decision making and leadership.

There are no quick fixes to improving the lives of students.

Marcal Graham, Ed.D

References

Aratani, L. 2006. "Upper Grades, Lower Reading Skills," *Washington Post*, July 13.

Babaraco, J. 2002. *Leading Quietly: An Unorthodox Guide to Doing the Right Thing.* Boston: Harvard Business School Press.

Bass, B., and R. Riggio. 2006. *Transformational Leadership.* Mahwah, New Jersey: Lawrence Erlbaum Associates Publishers.

Conley, D. 2007. "The Challenge of College Readiness." *Association for Supervision and Curriculum Development.* 64. no. 7 (April). Alexandria, Virginia.

Crawford, J. "A Diminished Vision of Civil Rights," *Education Week* 26, No. 39. (June 6).

Davis, G. 2007. "Minority Students Gaining on Gap." Baltimore Sun, (June 19, 2007) www.baltimore sun.com/news/local/baltimoresun.com/news/

local/baltimore_county/bal-md.co.scores15jun 15.0.19{June 19, 2007}.

Di Martino, J. & Castaneda, A. 2007. "Assessing Applied Skills." *Educational Leadership* 64, no. 7 (April).

Esquith, R. 2003. *There Are No Shortcuts*. New York: Anchor Books.

Gardner. H. 2006. *Five Minds for the Future*. Boston: Harvard Business School Press.

Gauld, L and M. Gauld. 2002. *The Biggest Job We'll Ever Have*. New York: Scribner.

Goffee, R., and G. Jones. 2000. *Why Should Anyone Be Led by You?* Boston: Harvard Business Review.

Grossman, K. 2007. "50 Million for what?" *Chicago Sun-Times*, May18. www.suntimes.com/news/education385515, CST-NWS-tutor15.article {May 18, 2007}

Hernandez, N. 2007. "With 2009 Test Mandate, Push to Prepare Students." *Washington Post*, March 8.

King, L. "Data Suggests States Satisfy No Child Law by Expecting Less of Students," *USA Today* {June 6, 2007} www.usatoday.com/news/education/2007-06-06-schools-main_N.htm{Accessed}

Kouzes, J., and B. Posner. 2002. *The Leadership Challenge*. San Francisco: Jossey-Bass.

Kozol, J. 2005. *The Shame of the Nation*: *The Restoration of Apartheid Schooling in America*. New York: Three Rivers Press.

Langemann, E. 2007. "Public Rhetoric, Public Responsibility, and the Public Schools." *Education Week* 26, no. 37 (May 16).

Levine, M. 2007. "The Essential Cognitive Backpack" *Educational Leadership* 64, no. 7 (April).

MacLeod, J. (1995). *Ain't No Makin' It: Aspirations & Attainment in a Low-Income Neighborhood*. Boulder: Westview.

Marzano, R. 2003. *What Works in Schools: Translating Research into Action*. Alexandria: Virginia. Association for Supervision and Curriculum Development.

Marx, G. 2006. *Future-Focused Leadership: Preparing schools, students, and communities for tomorrow's realities.* Alexandria Virginia: Association for Supervision and Curriculum Development.

Maxwell, J. 2006. *The Difference Maker.* Nashville: Nelson Business.

Noguero, P. 2003. *City Schools and the American Dream.* New York: Teachers College Press.

Paley, A. 2007. "Software's Benefits On Tests In Doubt." *The Washington Post*, April 5.

_____. 2007. "Test Scores at Odds With Rising High School Grades," *Washington Post*, February 23.

Sullo, B. 2007. *Activating the Desire to Learn.* Alexandria, Virginia: Association for Supervision and Curriculum Development.

Viadreo, D. (2007). "U.S. Rates Full Set of Character Education Programs," (www.edweek.org/ew/articles/2007/06/13/42character.h26.html?tmp=186101925)

(www2.edtrust.org; EDTrust/Press+Room/NAEP+
Grade+12.htmPaley, 2007).

About the Author

I am the product of what can happen if one is committed to excellence, hard work, discipline, and positive thinking. I have spent my life overcoming educational and professional obstacles even when people believed I could not achieve greatness. I attended traditional public schools all my K-12 life and earned my undergraduate degree in political science from La Salle University. After La Salle, I spent the next ten years of my life working on a masters in urban studies and a doctorate in educational administration from Temple University.

What I realize is that education is a life-long journey and passion that never stops!

978-0-595-45785-4
0-595-45785-1